William Young

Wishmaker's Town

Poems

William Young

Wishmaker's Town
Poems

ISBN/EAN: 9783744710282

Printed in Europe, USA, Canada, Australia, Japan

Cover: Foto ©Thomas Meinert / pixelio.de

More available books at **www.hansebooks.com**

Wishmakers' Town

By

William Young

With an Introductory Note by

Thomas Bailey Aldrich

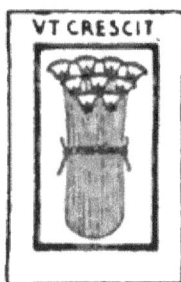

VT CRESCIT

Lamson, Wolffe and Company

Boston, New York and London

MDCCCXCVIII

Norwood Press
J. S. Cushing & Co.—Berwick & Smith
Norwood Mass. U.S.A.

CONTENTS

Introductory Note

A limited edition of this little volume of verse, which seems to me in many respects unique, was issued in 1885, and has long been out of print. The reissue of the book in its present form is in response to the desire of certain readers who have not forgotten the charm which the poem exercised upon them years ago, and, finding the charm still potent, would have others share it.

The scheme of the poem, for it is a poem and not simply a series of un-

related lyrics, is ingenious and origi-
nal, and unfolds itself in verse at once
strong and delicate, like silver wire.
The mood of the poet, and the method
of the playwright are obvious through-
out. Wishmakers' Town — a little
town situated in the no-man's-land
of The Tempest and A Midsummer
Night's Dream — is shown to us as it
awakens, touched by the dawn. The
clangor of bells far and near calls the
townfolk to their various avocations,
the toiler to his toil, the idler to his
idleness, the miser to his gold. In
swift and picturesque sequence the
dramatis personæ of the comedy

pass before us. Merchants, huxters,
players, lovers, gossips, soldiers, vaga-
bonds, and princes crowd the scene,
and have in turn their word of poig-
nant speech. We mingle with the
throng in the streets ; we hear the whir
of looms and the din of foundries,
the blare of trumpets, the whisper of
lovers, the scandals of the market-
place, and, in brief, are let into all the
secrets of the busy microcosm. A con-
tracted stage, indeed, yet large enough
for the play of many passions, as the
narrowest hearthstone may be. With
the sounding of the curfew, the town
is hushed to sleep again, and the cur-

tain falls on this mimic drama of life, this whimsical Masque of Man.

The charm of it all is not easily to be defined. Perhaps if one could name it, the spell were broken. Above the changing rhythms hangs an atmosphere too subtle and elusive for measurement — an atmosphere that stipulates an imaginative mood on the part of the reader. The quality which pleases in certain of the lyrical episodes is less intangible. One readily explains one's liking for so gracious a lyric as The Flower-Seller, to select an example at random. Next to the pleasure that lies

in the writing of such exquisite verse
is the pleasure of quoting it. I copy
the stanzas here, partly for my own
gratification, and partly to win the
reader to Wishmakers' Town, not
knowing better how to do it.

THE FLOWER-SELLER

Myrtle, and eglantine,
For the old love, and the new!
And the columbine,
With its cap and bells, for folly!
And the daffodil, for the hopes of youth!
    and the rue,
For melancholy!
But of all the blossoms that blow,

Fair gallants all, I charge you to win, if
  ye may,
This gentle guest,
Who dreams apart, in her wimple of purple
  and gray,
Like the blessed Virgin, with meek head
  bending low
Upon her breast.

For the orange flower
Ye may buy as ye will: but the violet of
  the wood
Is the love of maidenhood;
And he that hath worn it but once, though
  but for an hour,
He shall never again, though he wander by
  many a stream,
No, never again shall he meet with a flower
  that shall seem

So sweet and pure; and forever, in after
  years,
At the thought of its bloom, or the fragrance
  of its breath,
The past shall arise,
And his eyes shall be dim with tears,
And his soul shall be far in the gardens of
  Paradise,
Though he stand in the shambles of death.

I think there is a new generation
of readers for poetry in this kind,
and to them the book is commended.

The author of Wishmakers' Town
is the child of his period, and has not
escaped the maladie du siècle.
The doubt and pessimism that mark

the end of the century find a voice in the bell-like strophes with which the volume closes. It is the dramatist rather than the poet who speaks here. The real message of the poet to mankind is ever one of hope. Amid the problems that perplex and discourage, it is for him to sing

"Of what the world shall be
When the years have died away."

THOMAS BAILEY ALDRICH.

June, 1898.

Wishmakers' Town

I

THE BELLS

Voices

1

AWAKE! awake!
　　All living things that be,
In nest or fold!—
All lives that solace take,
And dreamful ease, in tent, or wind-blown
　　tree,
Or curtain'd couch, your wanderings forsake
In the dim realms of unreality!
　　　Awake, for shame
　　Of languor's soft delight!

1

Lo, once again earth's heaving disk is roll'd
   In rosy flame,
   And through the camps of night,
The flying Moon, beneath her splinter'd targe,
Sore-stricken by the feather'd shafts of Dawn,
And harried by her hounds, like Actæon,
         Kneels,
      Stoops, and wheels
   Adown the western marge !

               2

      Awake to toil !
   In wood, and rock-ribb'd hill,
      And loamy mead,
   What golden largess lies !
Awake to strife, and far-resounding deed,
In love's sweet quest, or honor's high emprise,
With trumpets blown, and clash of steed
   with steed !

Awake to care,
And triumph's frequent foil!
But still pursue! O hand with strength to
take —
O dauntless heart, to suffer, and to dare —
O swerveless will,
To bend, or else to break —
To life, to love, to conquest, and to spoil,
Awake! awake!

II

THE RINGERS

1

SEE the world of dome and spire —
　　How it gleams, and glows, and glistens,
In the Dawn's baptismal fire!
Whilst beneath us and around,
Quicken'd by the rain of sound,
Wakes the under-world, and listens.

2

— And the lark's far carol hear,
In the pauses of our clamor;
And the wheels, that far and near
Now their droning rounds begin;
And the market's busy din;
And the smiting of the hammer.

3

—Ah, the morn that once I knew,
When, with sweeter rapture shaken,
Sang the lark in yonder blue!—
Sang, and soared, the while I waited
For a sleeper, still belated,
With the waking world to waken!

4

—*Retro, retro, Sathanas!*
Vain unholy thoughts and fancies
Backward, backward, blend and pass!
Heaven shield and keep us free
From the wizard Memory,
And his cruel necromancies!

III

THE STROLLERS

Prologue

I

GOOD people, before ye turn
    To your follies, and plots, and treasons,
We pray you hear and behold
The whimsical Masque of Man,
Which shall here be acted and told
By your servants yclept THE SEASONS,
With its moral, which ye should learn,
For sundry and divers reasons,
And its melodies new and old,
Discoursed by the Pipes of Pan.

2

For we hold it timely and meet,
Thus, at the day's beginning,
To ask, in a mode debarr'd
To the pundits and the sages,
Whether the day's reward
Be properly worth the winning —
In short, if ye will, to treat
Of the current question of wages.

3

And so to your clemency
Do we yield us and address us,
With due humility;
And he that is overwise —
As some of you needs must be —
In damning us shall bless us,
For the opportunity
To cavil and criticise.

VERNALIS

Pray you, now, in your dance and rhyme,
Follow me deftly, in tune and time.

ÆSTIVUS

And prithee, piper, lower thy key,
Ever so little, if that may be.

AUTUMNUS

And mimic the windy woods and rills,
As well thou mayest, with fewer trills.

HIBERNUS

And time thy measures and suit thy tones,
Ever so little, to weary bones.

OMNES

Under the portals, and out, and in!
Now doth our roundel again begin.

IV

THE CHILDREN

WHO be these, in their strange array —
      Green, and russet, and brown, and gray —
Trick'd and tatter'd, and thus bedight,
Making merry for our delight? —
Out of the pictures on page and wall,
Come to revel or carnival?

Ho, for merry is he that leads,
Puffing his cheeks on the tuneful reeds,
And blowing and blowing with such a sound,
That out of the air, and out of the ground,
Birds and blossoms are whisk'd and whirl'd,
In flocks and bevies, along the world!

Ho, and merry is he that goes
Tripping the measure the piper blows! —
But ever and ever with shorter strides,
And panting, and holding his portly sides,
And marching and mincing, as one who could
Trip it forever, if but he would!

Nay, but merrier he, the next,
Who listens and listens, as half perplext,
And catches the measure, by times, per-
    chance,
And smiles, and simpers, and fain would
    dance,
And halts, and hobbles, and limps, and sighs,
And presses the kerchief against his eyes!

Trip, and amble, and shuffle past!
Ho, but the merriest yet, and last!

Trembling, tottering, how he feigns
Ever to writhe with aches and pains!
But well we know, by his beard of snow,
Him of the holly and mistletoe!

V

THE MAIDENS

TEACH us, witch-wife, as we pass,
   How to read the mystic roses.
Hold for us the magic glass,
   Which the coming face discloses.

VI

THE WITCH

HIM whose eyes rove everywhere,
  Like the moths that wheel and hover —
Pass him by, nor greatly care
  To be loved by such a lover.

But for him whose knitted brows
  Frown, in scorn of love and laughter —
She who wins him for a spouse,
  Shall be spoken of hereafter.

VII

THE MAIDENS

DIM, the warning! Choose we, then,
  Each for each; and, as a token,
Let the numbered leaves, again,
  Answer, when the choice is spoken.

BLUE EYES

I a sailor's bride will be.
  And, at night, upon my pillow,
The wind's voice shall seem to me
  As the roaring of the billow.

BROWN EYES

Pleasant be thy dreams, I pray.
  With a merchant will I marry:
Silks and pearls from far Cathay,
  Homeward all his ships shall carry.

BLACK EYES

And a soldier will I wed —
  Bold in love, and stern in duty.
When the tourney's lists are spread,
  He shall crown me Queen of Beauty.

GRAY EYES

Choose ye whom ye may and will!
  Though the king himself implore me,
I shall live unwedded still —
  And your husbands shall adore me.

VIII

THE STUDENTS

FOR the Graces and the Muses,
   Mourners, we, whom Fate abuses!
Yet, since woman now replaces
Both the Muses and the Graces,
Why not be content with her?
Gaudeamus igitur!

THE BOASTER

Book-worm, hast thou naught but scorning
For the blessings of the morning?
What avails it to be pat in
Musty Greek, or monkish Latin?

Here are volumes yet unread.
Heard'st thou what the Gray Eyes said?

THE MOCKER

Ay, and what a head she carries!
Woe, indeed, if e'er she marries!
Sure, I fancy, such a creature,
Trim of shape, and sleek of feature,
Led the dances, on the heights
Of the old Walpurgis nights.

THE BOASTER

Haply so; but prithee ponder
On her meeker sister, yonder.
Sweet it were, with ardor burning,
From far field or siege returning,
With a soldier's tale to sue
The fear-haunted Eyes of Blue.

THE IDLER

Sweet! — but sweeter yet, a rover,
Heedless of both fame and trover,
Over chartless seas to follow
Summer, with the flying swallow,
Glad, thro' Fortune's smile or frown,
With the merry Eyes of Brown!

THE EXEMPLAR

Only usefulness is beauty;
Yet, since marriage is a duty —
Yea, and since the eyes are witness
To its fitness or unfitness,
And my own some luster lack,
I shall mate with Orbs of Black.

THE BOASTER

Where is he, who in derision
Of the Gray first gave decision?

THE IDLER

Heed him not: 'tis but his fashion
To decry the tender passion.

THE EXEMPLAR

Mark him, yonder, o'er the way,
Bowing to the Eyes of Gray!

IX

THE FLOWER-SELLER

MYRTLE, and eglantine,
  For the old love, and the new !
And the columbine,
With its cap and bells, for folly !
And the daffodil, for the hopes of youth !
  and the rue,
For melancholy !
But of all the blossoms that blow,
Fair gallants all, I charge you to win, if ye
  may,
This gentle guest,
Who dreams apart, in her wimple of purple
  and gray,

Like the blessed Virgin, with meek head
    bending low
Upon her breast.

For the orange flower
Ye may buy as ye will: but the violet of
    the wood
Is the love of maidenhood ;
And he that hath worn it but once, though
    but for an hour,
He shall never again, though he wander by
    many a stream,
No, never again shall he meet with a flower
    that shall seem
So sweet and pure ; and forever, in after
    years,
At the thought of its bloom, or the fragrance
    of its breath,

The past shall arise,
And his eyes shall be dim with tears,
And his soul shall be far in the gardens of
    Paradise,
Though he stand in the shambles of death.

X

THE TRIFLERS

HE

BECAUSE thou wast cold and proud,
　　And as one alone in the crowd,
And because of thy willful and wayward
　　look,
I thought, as I saw thee above my book,
" I will prove if her heart be flesh or stone."
And in seeking thine, I have found my own.

SHE

Because thou wast proud and cold,
And because of the story told
That never had woman a smile from thee,

I thought, as I glanced, " If he frown on me,
Why, be it so! but his peace shall atone."
And in troubling thine, I have lost my own.

XI

THE CONFIDANTE

SAY, dost thou love him?—O love, love,
   love !
   How should I know what thy wild words
      mean ?
— But *dost* thou love him?— As God's above,
   The man I shall wed I have not yet seen !

— But why, if yes, shouldst thou not con-
   fess ?
   — And why, if no, may I not deny ?
— Or, whether the answer be no or yes,
   Wilt thou trust me no more, as in days
      gone by ?

For why, but now, when I named his name —
  The name that thy lips have learn'd to
  shun —
Was thy cheek, in hue, like the poppy's
  flame?
  And why dost thou dream in the noon-day
  sun?

And sister, my sister — for such thou art —
  O, where dost thou walk, in the evenings
  dim?
And why hast thou cast me out of thy heart?
  And, prithee, for whom, if not for him?

— O, sister, my sister, — for wilt thou be,
  In truth, my sister? — believe me well:
That I hate myself and love but thee,
  Is the only secret I have to tell.

XII

THE MASKERS

So soon! so soon! Ah, go not yet!
— Alas, the day whereon we met!

— Accurst be he who doubts between
The rose-leaf and the laurel green!

— And yet, for him who doubts, 'tis plain
The fairest rose might bloom in vain.

— Art thou so wise? Then be it so!
Yet one last kiss! — Ah, no! ah, no!

— No kiss, no kiss, to comfort me?
— Think on the last I gave to thee!

— Nor yet to hold thy hand in mine?
— Farewell, farewell, without a sign!

— And when to meet? — Pray God, no more,
On the dark river's hither shore!

— Nor yet beyond? — Ah, who shall tell?
But, for this world, farewell, farewell!

XIII

THE HAWKER

COME, buy!—Come, buy!—Come, buy!
  Ho! people of all degrees,
And honors and dignities,
And stations both low and high!
So that your purses be long,
And the ring of your coin be true,
There is never a wrong so wrong,
That it shall not be reckon'd a right,
At your behest, and for you
The green shall be green, or be blue,
And the blackest of black shall be white.

For 'tis proper to woo, and to wed,
And betimes to build castles in Spain —
And to see them demolish'd again —
And 'tis proper to bury the dead:
And for all things under the sun,
There hath been, and shall be a time,
And a due and appropriate season.
"For all things," said I?— Save one!
There is never a time for rhyme,
And but seldom a season for reason:
And ye, within sound of my voice,
To whom Fortune — the jade !— hath been
    cold,
In matters of love or ambition,
Be advis'd, and before ye berate her,
And consign yourselves straight to perdition,
Entreat her again to a choice:
But rely on a talisman greater
Than reason, or rhyme — to wit, GOLD.

GOLD! GOLD! Though the poet may sing,
And the moralist preach and proclaim,
'Tis the stuff that gives worth to the ring;
'Tis the stuff that gives weight to the name.
It shall bind — it shall loose — it shall break:
It shall sunder the bridegroom and bride,
And shall laugh at the bigots who chide:
It shall pick — it shall choose — it shall take:
It shall use, and refuse; and the charms
For which Merit and Virtue have striven,
It shall give to the lecher's foul arms,
If it will! And, in fine, brief to tell,
To have it, and hold it, is Heaven!
And to lack it, or lose it, is Hell!

But what! do I hear you protest,
'Tis the want of the means to apply it,
That robs my discourse of its zest?

And for this have we churches, and schools,
And a code that was specially plann'd
For the definite purpose! O fools!—
For if poor, ye were wise to deny it—
Is there one of you here, as ye stand,
Who hath not a friend, or a neighbor,
With some little treasure in store—
Some pitiful profit of labor,
Which is lonely and fruitless, unmated,
And which, by the methods devis'd,
May be legally aggregated,
And properly capitalized?
Yea, saith not the Good Book itself—
And its language is not to be shaken,
In the veriest tittle or jot—
Saith it not, on the subject of pelf,
That he who hath, shall have more;
Whilst from him who hath not,
That which he hath shall be taken?

Wherefore, with traffic and barter,
I bid you make haste to fulfill
The Scriptural injunction;
And to plunder, at your sweet will,
Whilst ye quote from the recognized charter,
With the proper degree of unction.

XIV

THE CONSCIENCE-KEEPER

REPENT, O ye, predestinate to woe!
  'Tis mine to cry — albeit, well I wis,
Ye may not heed. And ye, elect to bliss,
Must e'en be saved, whether I cry or no.

And yet, repent! Repent ye, and atone,
  In either case. Forswear your wisdom's
    pride,
  And pray for faith — though some must
    be denied!
Nor yet by prayer, nor yet by faith alone,

But by your works, attest your penitence.
  Give to the poor!— of whom ye see in me
  God's almoner — and in your charity,
Deign to forget not Peter and his pence.

XV

THE PRODIGAL

EACH in his turn, good brother!
  For I hold it a vicious practice
For two of a trade to compete,
Where the pickings, at best, are but small —
As here they seem. — And the fact is
That the odds are but prattle and pother,
'Twixt the beads that are sold in the street,
And the beads that are told in the stall.

For what hath the vender to vend,
Save the remnants and tokens of blisses,
To make the mouth water and pine?
And what, though in absolute truth,

The pledge be confirm'd, that is penn'd,
And the next world be fairer than this is?—
Yet, O, for the wine—for the wine
Of the glorious vintage of youth!

O, subtler and sweeter than honey!—
Than the honey of storied Hymettus!
O, rare as the perfumes of Ind!—
What to us were the raptures to be,
Or the saddest of sins we have sinn'd,
Or the sins that at present beset us,
Or the want, or the worship of money,
Dulcet wine, could we tarry with thee?

Woe is me!—But when spent is thy savor,
We must needs be both sober and ruthful:
And so, in my garments of sacking,
Let me taste of the waters Divine!—

Since their cheapness is now in their favor,
And even though spice may be lacking,
Were not veal, in its season, more toothful
Than a handful of husks with the swine!

XVI

THE WORKERS

WHAT is this, that we build?
— It is Wealth's strong tower:
And, when it is finished, the people shall
throng to see;
And the kings of the earth shall cringe be-
fore it, and cower —
Saith the master.
— Ay? — But where, then, shall *we* be?

XVII

THE MONEY-CHANGERS

WHAT news from the East?
  —Good news! The Venetian, again,
In despite of the truce, hath been bow-
    string'd by the Turk.
—And the Pope and the Emperor, now,
    shall hardly abstain
From the savory broil.
—There is like to be murderous work!
—And, moreover, 'tis said that in certain
    broad districts of France,
Where the drouth hath prevail'd, there will
    scarce be a mouthful of bread,
To the good square league.

— And, by those most observant, 'tis said
Our own crops must be short!
— Then, at once, we may look for advance
Both in rates of per cent., and in prices of
    fuel and food?
— Why, so I conclude, from the signs that
    at present appear;
And at once shall distrain on all forfeited
    bonds.
— God is good!
And to Him be the praise! We have need
    of a prosperous year.

XVIII

THE CHESS-PLAYERS

NEIGHBOR of mine, no malice I bear,
But pawns and pieces must earn their
fare ;

And time hangs heavy.   So, red or white,
Choose thy color, and pitch thy fight.

— Little the color concerneth me,
But say now, what shall the wager be?

Lands, or vassals, or good red gold ?
— Lands, I prithee ; and all is told.

For quickly that which the coffer lacks
May be recruited, with toll and tax;

And he that payeth the tax is thrall;
And the lord of the land is the lord of all.

— Good! Have at thee! And, overhead,
Guard me Heaven, and help the Red!

— And Thou, to the glory of whom I fight,
Father of mercies, befriend the White!

XIX

THE PAWNS

PRINCE, and Bishop, and Knight, and
      Dame,
   Plot, and plunder, and disagree!
O but the game is a royal game!
   O but your tourneys are fair to see!

None too hopeful we found our lives;
   Sore was labor from day to day;
Still we strove for our babes and wives —
   Now, to the trumpet, we march away!

"Why?"—For some one hath will'd it so!
  Nothing we know of the why or the
    where—
To swamp, or jungle, or wastes of snow—
  Nothing we know, and little we care.

Give us to kill!—since this is the end
  Of love and labor in Nature's plan;
Give us to kill and ravish and rend,
  Yea, since this is the end of man.

States shall perish, and states be born:
  Leaders, out of the throng, shall press;
Some to honor, and some to scorn:
  We, that are little, shall yet be less.

Over our lines shall the vultures soar;
  Hard on our flanks shall the jackals cry;

And the dead shall be as the sands of the
    shore ;
    And daily the living shall pray to die.

Nay, what matter! — When all is said,
    Prince and Bishop will plunder still:
Lord and Lady must dance and wed.
    Pity us, pray for us, ye that will!

XX

THE GOSSIPS

SO, the usurer's son hath return'd,
    and will take to himself a wife!
Thou art bid to the feast, good neighbor?
    —I cry thee mercy! Not I!
There are those who have too much knowl-
    edge
    of a certain page, in the life
Of the bride, in the days of her girlhood.
    But by-gones should be gone by.

— " Of the bride," dost thou say? Now truly,
    of her lord-and-master-elect,

I have heard what is told from the house-
top ;
but better the prodigal son,
Than the daughter who hath a secret !
And would'st thou have me suspect—?
—Marry, go to ! Shall I tell thee ?
But I charge thee repeat it to none.

For marvelous strange is the story ;
and great is its hero, forsooth !
And well, of old, didst thou know him,
in his student's cap, when he came,
With his fellows, under the lindens —
and we thought him a callow youth !
And there it was that she met him —
and I leave thee to guess his name.

And there it was that she met him —
how well I recall the morn !

And once — but once — from the volume,
    that seem'd his only delight,
He look'd, and their cold eyes counter'd,
    with glances of equal scorn: —
And each in the self-same pathway
    wander'd, again, at night.

But dost thou look for the wherefore,
    that made of the twain a pair?
I can think of it but as the spirit
    that sets the lances a-tilt:
Yet I count it a happy fortune —
    and I would it were not so rare —
That matches the born deceiver
    with her that is born a jilt!

Be that as it may, he was master —
    though she ever denied the yoke —
But daily her glance was troubled,
    and her step grew feeble, and slow;

Till what with the strain, or the chafing,
    the something that bound them broke:
  And, seeing him fain to desert her,
      she was fain to say to him, "Go!"

And she came to me, white from the struggle,
    for I was her dearest friend:
  But she stood before me defiant,
      though the salt-drop well'd in her
      eye;
For pride was ever her failing —
    and so it will be to the end;
  And she told me the truth, in a measure;
    and in part she told me a lie:

And prank'd herself in her finest,
    and was gay, again, with the gay —
  Bold, and simple, and subtle,
    and gay as never before;

Till the stale, lack-luster suitor,
    from the great house over the way,
  Nursing his kindred secret,
    in due time, came to the door.

Came — and while yet she ponder'd,
    a breath was blown from the wars —
  Rumors of siege and conquest;
    and the streets first thrill'd with
    the name
That had once been hers — in her fancy —
    and we listen'd, under the stars,
  To the sound of the herald's trumpet —
    the terrible trumpet of Fame.

Then I, that was witness, noted
    how the pale lips quiver'd and met,
  And the proud eye dimm'd, for a moment,
    with a moisture, never so slight;

And I said, " It is wise, sweet sister;
     as thou art forgotten, forget!"
And even for this — wouldst thou think
     it ? —
        hath the vixen held me in spite.

Yea, even for this! But, God save us,
     I would that the words were unsaid!
And if, to thee, she was stainless,
     why let her be stainless still!
Nay, yet must I thank my Maker,
     who hath spared me the wish to wed.
And I pray that their lives may be happy —
     but that must be as it will.

XXI

THE BRIDAL PAIR

HE

THOUGH the roving bee, as lightly,
  Sip the sweets of thyme and clover,
Though the moon of May, as whitely,
  Silver all the greensward over,
    Yet, beneath the trysting tree,
    That hath been which shall not be!

SHE

Drip the viols, ne'er so sweetly,
  With the honey-dew of pleasure —
Trip the dancers, ne'er so featly,
    Through the old remembered measure,
      Yet, the lighted lanthorn round,
      What is lost shall not be found!

XXII

THE PHILOSOPHERS

THE PESSIMIST

GOD of our fathers! what monstrous birth
　　Out of the loins of To-day shall spring,
To trample the fruitful fields of earth,
　　And pluck the flower, and wear the ring?

For the parent barters the child for gold;
　　And the bidder bids with a jest and a leer;
And the shameless daughter is fain to be
　　sold;
　　But he that buys her shall find her dear!

And yet, what fitness — what righteous grace,
  In such a union! Since time began,
The sexes have journeyed with equal pace,
  And the woman is still but the mate of
    the man!

THE OPTIMIST

What does the cynic mutter about?
  Mark him there, in his sable gown,
Like a specter, threading the rout,
  Ever with sidelong stare and frown!

Once, together, we woo'd a maid:
  "Which of the twain did her heart pre-
    fer?"
Deep, the riddle! Our court we paid:
  Pale he turn'd, at her soft demur:

Willy-nilly, I took the kiss!
  Which is the richer, he or I?
Which of us will she mourn or miss,
  A day the longer, after we die?

THE NAMELESS

Yonder is he, who taught me, first,
  The steps that lead to the pit of flame.
Merry, the jest! Be his soul accurst!
  Lives he in honor, and I in shame?

And yonder, dreaming his one sad dream,
  Is he, with whom, in his robes of woe,
Spake he the word, over death's dark
    stream,
  Willingly, gladly would I go.

Lovers I count on my finger-tips ;
  Lives, like dice, for my smiles are thrown ;
Still, forever, upon my lips,
  Burns the kiss I never have known !

XXIII

THE GIFT-BEARERS

HEAR us, Dives! — Gifts we bring
  For thy first-born's christening.

Hear! — And these, our treasures, see!
Nard, and all sweet spicery!
And the subtle frankincense,
That shall woo and waft thee hence,
Into regions long forbid
To the dream-affrighted lid! —
Breathe! nor longer fear to dream,
Lapsing with the lapsing stream —

Lapsing with the tide that ebbs,
Till the shallops' sheeny webs
Peer again above the blue,
Steering, veering, and the hue
Of the sapphire sea is blent
With the sapphire firmament.

Search, and sail, and tack, and veer!
Nay, the drowsy noon is near. —
What be these that float and lie
Half in sea, and half in sky?
Islands, or the misty shapes
Of the Cloud-land's phantom capes?
Surely, surely, fairer, these,
Than the far Hesperides!
Search, and find, and prove, and know!
Welcome weal or welcome woe!
Fear not thou the glimpses brief

Of the vainly charted reef —
Nor the sea-shell, blown, for tryst,
Through the languors of the mist —
Nor the navies, long unmann'd,
Where they whiten on the strand —
Nor the veiling tresses, stirr'd
With the song Ulysses heard.

———

Grecian, Grecian, wast thou wise? —
Passer with averted eyes ! —
Broken are the myths; and fled,
From Olympus, overhead,
God and goddess; yea, and these,
Dwellers by the shoaling seas,
Though they linger, linger still —
Charmers of the weary will,
Whatsoever winds may blow —
Mortal, as thyself, we know.

WISHMAKERS' TOWN

Mortal — by the lips that pine ! —
Neither demon, nor divine !
By the fervor of the kiss —
Yea, and dear because of this !
By the transport of the tear —
And, because of this, more dear !
By all tokens sweet and fair —
By the bold limbs, flashing bare !
By the lock's dishevel'd curl !
By the parted teeth of pearl,
With the beaker spill'd between,
Rarer than the Hippocrene !
— Up ! the mazy dance is wound,
To the viol's vibrant sound,
And the cithern's smitten string ;
Faster, closer, pant and cling :
Till the wheel within the wheel
Of the brain begins to reel —
Till the heaving bosoms show,

As they heave, and as they glow,
Like the leper's spotted o'er;
And the wine becomes as gore;
And the sick gorge quivers up,
At the dregs within the cup!

Break, and blend, and fade, and change!
And, again, the streaming range
Of the salt-waste, dipping far,
To a night without a star!
And Æolus, harping loud,
On the sheet and on the shroud!
And Charybdis on the lee —
By the levin, dread to see —
Roaring through the cloudy rack!
Hark! — And Scylla yelping back!
Till, at last, upon the ken,
Rimm'd with lifting lights again,

Lo, the welcome, welcome shore!
Chasten'd spirit, fare no more:
Scorn of self is noble scorn.
Wake!—It is thy marriage-morn!

O, the censer's musky breath!
O, the bride who lingereth!
O, the chanting of the psalm;
And the organ's holy calm;
And the brides-maids pacing slow;
And the great bell, to and fro,
Yearning, turning, till the word
From the laggard lips be heard!
—Doth she answer?—Lift the veil!
Marble!—marble, cold, and pale!—
Stilly, faultless, chisel'd fine!—
Claim thy purchase—all is thine.
Claim her; use her to thy will.

To thy kisses, marble, still ! —
Kisses neither met nor spurn'd,
But received, and unreturn'd !
— " Stilly, chilly, Death-in-Life,
Who is he should call thee wife ? "
— Doubling, troubling, damnéd doubt,
Shall not searching find thee out ? —
In the speech, or in the glance ? —
In the features' stony trance ? —
Naught of pleasure, naught of pain ;
Only passionless disdain !
Saving when the Springtime calls,
From the wood beyond the walls —
Then the answer in the eye,
That forever looks thee by !
Then the tremor of the hand,
That thou canst not understand !
Turn thee, turn thee ! Know, at last,
Something fair is overpast —

WISHMAKERS' TOWN

Something! — reck not greatly what:
Here is other food for thought.
Let thy latest love be told
In the chime of gold on gold!

———————

Hurry! worry! warp and weft,
Spread the toils of thrift and theft;
Parchment pit-falls, and the wiles
Of the ledger's mouldy files.
Garner malice, garner fear;
Yet the world shall hold thee dear.
Garner envy, garner scorn —
Unto thee, a son is born!
— "O, thou Blossom, dear above
Every pledge of fancied love! —
For, though loveless, shalt thou be
Surety of the fruitful tree.
Yet, I wonder, wilt thou list

When the ready curse is hiss'd
At the breathing of my name?
Wilt thou praise, or wilt thou blame?
Wilt thou redden, cheek and brow?
O, but love me!—only thou!
For my soul is sick of hate—
Comfortless, and desolate.
Now for thee I heap and hoard.''
—Bid the feasters to thy board!
Gather! gather!—What is here?
Shapes of doubt, and shapes of fear—
Specters, laid with book and bell—
Madness, from its padded cell—
Lo, and here a throat that bleeds!
And the widow's scanty weeds,
Ever closer wrapp'd and press'd,
For a shelter, at her breast
Round the something stark and wan
That thou may'st not look upon!

WISHMAKERS' TOWN

— Make obeisance, sigh, and glance;
Peep, and mutter, and advance;
Leer, and ogle, and retreat;
Hither, thither, cross and meet —
Brightest eyes may glimmer dull,
From the sockets of a skull.
— Is not this a fit carouse,
For the heir to such a house? —
Heir apparent, after thee,
To this goodly company —
To the sharp-tooth'd rats that gnaw,
Nightly, at the coffer's flaw;
And the look that stabs thee — thus,
Through the eyes of Lazarus!
— Haste! — The turrets topple all,
Reeling to their windy fall.
Clatter! chatter! hands about!
Curvet in the ribald rout!
"*Mercy!*" dost thou cry! — But, nay,

Shall not JUSTICE have her day?
O, before the sands be run,
Be the knavery undone!
From thee, from thee, rend and cast
Like a garment, all the Past—
Garment, foul with smear and smutch;
And thy bony fingers' clutch
Loosen!—and thy bleeding nails,
From thy bolts and from thy bales!—
From the plunder of the hearth,
From the acres of the earth,
Hardly won, and gloated on,
Through the dusk and through the dawn!
O, before the round be sped,
To the quick, and to the dead,
Yield, and render, and restore!
—Peace!—The bier is at the door.

XXIV

THE MOTHER

WHY did I bring thee, Sweet,
 Into a world of sin?—
Into a world of wonder, and doubt,
With sorrow and snares for the little white
 feet—
Into a world, whence the going out
Is as dark as the coming in!

XXV

THE WANDERER

JOINER, joining the oaken seam,
  All so lonely, and dusty gray,
Shaking thy head, in a waking dream,
  Where be thy fellows of yesterday?

—Past and gone from the trodden sill;
  Each on his errand: and all for naught!
For men are coming and going still;
  But still must the joiner's task be
    wrought.

—Why, well thou sayest, thou mournful
   wight!
But dost thou remember the students four,
Who sang, of old, in the waning light
   Of the golden evenings, before thy door?

—And do I remember? And wast thou one
   Of that boastful band?—For mine eyes
   are dim.
Nay! for with tempest, and foreign sun,
   Scarr'd thou seemest, and swarth and
   grim!

And fair were they; and they vowed their
   vows;
   And the maidens listen'd, in hut and hall;
And still they talked, as they held carouse,
   Of what should happen and what befall:

And one must rail at the miser's greed:
  And he of them, only, hath learn'd to
    hoard!
And one should win, with the poet's screed,
  What he hath won with the victor's
    sword!

And one should journey beyond the foam;
  And never his eyes beheld the sea!
And one of them, only, should bide at
    home;
  And half I fancy that thou art he!

—O vex thee not with the plans I plann'd;
  But tell me!—what of thy daughter
    fair?
And wears she a ring on the lily hand,
  So smooth and slender beyond compare?

For here be jewels of East and West,
  And here be spoils of the Southern shell,
Won, with danger, at love's behest,
  And who is the giver, her heart shall tell.

—Now what, to thee, is her lily hand?
  And what, to thee, was her love so dear?
And how shall she care for thy jewels
    grand,
  Now that her coffin I fashion here?

—Why, truly, truly, if these things be,
  There is never a solace for those that
    roam,
In all that their slumbering eyes may see,
  More false than the dreams of the coming-
    home.

XXVI

THE WATCHERS

NAY, but hark!   Dost thou hear?
    And again!
—Like the sough of the wind!
—Or the thunder!
—Or the steadily on-coming, gathering rush
    of the rain!
—Or the surges that grind
On the sheer
Scarpéd cliffs of the main,
With the hoarse caverns bellowing under!
—Yet at peace are the skies.

—Yea, and fair
Is the ripening earth. And behold!
Is yon but the creeper, that trails from the
    spur of the crag?—
But the ripple of crimson, that heralds the
    Autumn, and flies,
With the raven and chough, from the vale-
    guarding crest of the wold?
—Nay! What, but the flare
Of the death-dripping, wind-flutter'd flag,
As it writhes, and advances, with tortuous
    fold upon fold!
—To the gates! to the gates!
It is he!
It is he, who, in triumph, from fields red
    with slaughter and sown
With the teeth of the Dragon—fell pledges
    of harvests to be!—
Now returns to his own!

And the profits we may not espy,

But we welcome him back, with the brood
    of the Furies and Hates,

That attend on his steps: and we know not
    the cause, but we cry,

As to Cæsar of old, *Be our praise! be our
homage to thee!*

To the bells!

Let them rock, let them reel,

Over roof-tree and dome!

And the balconied gables, arow,

Let them burgeon and blossom with stuffs
    of the Orient loom! —

With the hues of the gardens of Schiraz!
    — And traffic, below,

With its burdensome wheel,

Let it cease from the pave, and make room

For the march of the Brave! —

For the multiple murmur that tells

Of the march of the Brave,

As it winds, as it sinks, as it swells,

And resounds, and out-bursts in the cannon's
far-shattering peal!

For behold where he comes! — And the
daughters of Beauty, unclad,

Let them glimmer before him, with timbrel
and tabor, and sing

Of the fame of his deeds! — Let us shout,
let us leap, and be glad!

*Thou hast conquer'd our foes! Thou hast rid us
of kings!* — BE THOU KING!

XXVII

THE VICTOR

BLARE of trumpet, and roll of drum!
Hath the day of my fancy come?

Dimly the house-tops seem to sway,
Over the mile-long crowded way

To the palace portals: and hark!—the cry,
"Hail to the victor, who passes by!"

Banner and pennon flutter red,
Dyed with the blood that my hands have
    shed;

And red and white are the roses strewn
Under my horse's silver shoon:

But O, for the face that I do not see,
In casement, or in balcony!

Hides she there, where the shadows lurk,
Under the awnings of needle-work?—

Silent, and pale, with her white hands
    press'd
Over the tumult of her breast?—

Stands she to gaze?—And her eyes, forlorn,
Look they in hatred, or pride, or scorn?

Onward! neither to left, nor right,
Let me glance, in the rabble's sight!

Neither by word nor sign, reveal
The sad, sick brain, in the casque of steel!

Empty pageant, and passing show!
Thus doth the day of my fancy go!

These, the guerdon of love's duress —
Pain, and peril, and weariness!

Better, mayhap, if the foeman's spear
Under my cuirass were buried here!

Better, if now, through the gala town,
Heralded thus, I were riding down,

As the sweet Saints grant that I soon may
   ride,
Shrouded, and shriven, and satisfied!

Yea, that I never had heard the cry,
"Hail to the victor, who passes by!"

XXVIII

THE BELLS

Voices

I

FORBEAR! forbear!
    The midges' dance is spun.
O fool of Time,
That, with thy puny powers,
Did'st dream, within the circuit of the Sun,
To prove the promise of our matin chime—
    Thy task forswear,
    For lo, the darkness lowers!

Thy task forswear,
For lo, the day is done!
O, fool of Time—
Whose voice is one with ours!

2

The day is done!
Now quake with all thy fears.
Thy soul, how often, to the passing bell,
The pall, the plume,
Hath falter'd forth in tears!—
In sighs profound,
And shudder'd on the blast,
Yea, but to think upon thy coming knell!
Now it doth sound!—
Are all thy terrors past?
Now it doth sound!
Now yawns the vasty gloom!

And, tearless now, the brink thou dost not
    shun?
—O Riddle, deeper even than thy doom,
What hope is thine, that thou dost smile
    at last?

3

In vain is toil!—
To sow, and not to reap!
The thankless earth
Becomes the delver's grave.
In vain is strife!—to win, and not to keep!
The trickster grasps the laurels of the brave;
And Craft, in turn, to Folly yields its spoil—
In vain is love!—
To plight and then to part!
And still to wear the galling mask of mirth!
To know the ill, all other ills above,
That mocks the venom of the Slayer's dart,

With subtler pain!
O soul, fore-doomed from birth!
O toil-worn brain!
O eyes, long used to weep!—
Yet now ye smile?—Then we, too, are in vain!
To sleep!—to sleep!

FINIS